Poetry FROM Christ

Poetry FROM Christ

PRACTICING FAITH

June Pierce-Hampton

authorHOUSE®

AuthorHouse™
1663 Liberty Drive
Bloomington, IN 47403
www.authorhouse.com
Phone: 1-800-839-8640

Published by AuthorHouse 11/05/2014

ISBN: 978-1-4969-4950-9 (sc)
ISBN: 978-1-4969-4949-3 (e)

KJV
Scripture quotations marked KJV are from the Holy Bible, King James Version (Authorized Version). First published
in 1611. Quoted from the KJV Classic Reference Bible, Copyright © 1983 by The Zondervan Corporation.

CONTENTS

ACKNOWLEDGEMENT

First and foremost, I want to thank our living GOD for using me as an instrument to write poetry on and in HIS behalf. It is only through our Heavenly Father these poems are in existence, copyrighted and published. Thank you JESUS!!

Baron C. Whitaker brought my attention to a powerful prayer line; which I joined March 2013, thank you Baron.

The Prayer line is hosted by Bishop Edward C. Gresham, Monday through Friday, beginning at 6:45 a.m.; the phone number for those who would like to join is: 1-530-881-1212 (code 119 540 355 #), EST. There is no cost when using cell phones. I give my gratitude to Bishop Gresham for such a spiritual awakening and uplift each morning during the week.

To Sister Young, who began reading poetry on the prayer line, I want to acknowledge her and thank Sister Young for her inspiration, which encouraged me to begin my journey for this manuscript.

My daughters, De'Anginae' Nicole Mares-Zavala (first born) and Tiffany Elizabeth Hampton (last born); I love you both with all my heart and soul! Know that as long as you believe and trust in GOD, everything is alright!

GOD sent Ira (Tony) and Brenda Rouse to assist with the proofing of this manuscript. I thank GOD for sending them to my rescue, which they did with sincere love and grace. Thanks so much!

Last but not least, to my six grandchildren: Brittani Maria, Brook-Lynn June, Pierce Bernard, Asaryia Ginae, Nicoleus Mitchel and little Jewl Tracy. I love you all very much!

ABOUT THE AUTHOR

June has experienced life's trials and tribulations since her mother passed March 1968. June was only 14 years of age. Her daddy remarried only three months after her mother's death, which was extremely traumatic. As her parent's only child, she was extremely overprotected prior to her mother's passing. Naïve entering into young adulthood, June found solace in reading the bible and exercising its teachings, which her mother had taught her. As life presented obstacles, June's faith increased. Real life miracles began to happen with no explanation other than GOD ALMIGHTY watching over her. One can tell by reading her poetry, her faith increased exponentially during this darkest period of her life. A few of those trials include homelessness; financial ruin when the real estate market declined; home totally loss during the 2009 floods of northern Georgia. Many, many more obstacles occurred, which are too much to recall, but GOD always came through!

June was widowed and left fatherless in March 2002, when both her husband and daddy transitioned from earth the same month and year. Her grief was insurmountable. She asked GOD, "Why did you take my mother, my daddy, and my husband all in the month of March"? GOD answered her question immediately, HIS reply, "because you must continue to march, march, march on to make it to MY throne. Do what is good, trust totally in ME, and then you will see all your loved ones again." Needless to say, the grief went away instantly. June knew what GOD told her was true!

June is a Georgia Licensed Real Estate agent and has been in the profession over 30 years. June also volunteers with the Hospice program in her community. The poetry is directed from JESUS through her. June would be given subjects to write, with pen and paper GOD gave her the words for **Poetry from Christ!**

THANK YOU JESUS FOR THIS DAY!

Thank you Jesus for this day; we all awoke ready to pray!
Giving you praise as we start a fresh new day.

Our faith is strong as you can see, giving you praise humbly, lead and guide us in your special way as we progress through this day.

Take us through this day with Trust – we know in our hearts you will protect us – for you are the Greatest the world has known and we all want to make it to your Throne.

We thank you Jesus for your love and showering us with your gifts from above -- your power is awesome in every way, just waking us up another day.

You are the light that we shall seek; keep us humbled, mild and meek as days turn into weeks.

Thank you GOD for your grace and another day that we will face.

Amen!

Ephesians 5:20

BASIC INSTRUCTIONS BEFORE LEAVING EARTH
(BIBLE)

Through the scriptures HE left the world with HIS instructions on how to live life without destruction!

HIS words are true from the beginning to the end; HE teaches us how to live and not to sin!

HE instructs us to have Faith in HIM through thick and thin and to always keep that Faith deep within.

HE tells us to obey his **commandments**, stay prayed up, trust in HIM then it will be easier to handle all disappointments.

The Bible is a source of knowledge -- providing strength, faith, and grace, secure in knowing the **LORD cannot lie** for us to find peace on earth before we die!

So I say, read the Bible because it is surely "**B**asic **I**nstructions **B**efore **L**eaving **E**arth", follow HIS words to the end, find peace within!

Amen!

Proverbs 12:1

WHY ARE WE HERE!

Why are we here? The Bible it says we should never FEAR! For trusting and believing the LORD is always near!

Why are we here? To Praise our God, to Love our God to thank our GOD, with cheer!

Why are we here? To love one another, to help one another, to inspire one another, to honor one another and to be sincere!

Why are we here? To make the choices GOD commands us to make, the ones that HE whispers in our ear!

Why are we here? To allow GOD to lead and guide us in the way HE have us to go, here on earth to serve HIM all day in every way and strive to be united with GOD on HIS throne, thereby rebuking satan and doing nothing wrong!

WE ARE HERE to serve our MASTER with all our hearts mind and soul, and with that our spirits will remain **HEALTHY, HOLY AND BOLD**!

Amen!

Psalms 37:11

REVELATIONS 12:12

Clearly tell us that evil has been cast out of Heaven and now is on earth; this verse is true beginning with our birth.

This is a warning for all mankind to take heave and prepare -- for evil is on the earth to cause downright despair.

When we Trust in the LORD with all our minds, heart and soul, it will be proven GOD still has control.

When evil surrounds our thoughts and being, we must get on our knees and pray; GOD can work it out in HIS gracious way.

GOD has given us the freedom of choice, to honor HIM and praise HIM with our mind, time and our voice.

Take HIS commandments very serious—that's why HE left them for all our experiences.

Know and understand that GOD's hand is on our shoulder and with that knowledge it makes us wiser and bolder.

Establish a personal relationship with GOD to protect you from the evil in the land; it is truly the only way to keep protection close at hand!
Amen!

Revelation 12:12

OCCUPING OUR MINDS

Occupy your minds thinking of GOD'S grand designs; HE created the universe for all mankind; wanting the earth as our paradise for all time.

The sun, the moon, the stars, the birds, the flowers and the rain showers are just a few of HIS awesome creations, these things comes together for HIS relationship with human mankind.

When we see mankind created in HIS likeness, yet so different -- we know his creation should never bring about separation; it should be viewed as a spiritual preparation.

Preparation to make it to HIS Throne, and how in the world do we think we'll get there by doing and thinking things that are obviously wrong.

Keep in mind of the love HE has for us all – not to have wars – not to hurt, maim nor murder one another; that is not HIS direction for the earth as we all begin this journey from birth.

Occupy your mind with **peace love and grace**; occupy your mind with the **Lord in every place**!

Amen.

Luke 2:14

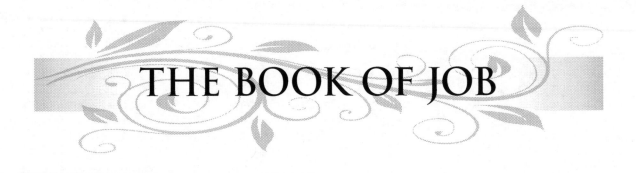

THE BOOK OF JOB

Job was tested like no other – GOD left the book of Job in the bible for all to see, we can overcome hardships and hard times, but it will not be easy for you or me.

Being tested in our faith is part of life – when we pass the test of trials and tribulations more will be upon us and attempt to cause strife and even destroy our life.

Job has shown us when our faith is strong in GOD, strife will not become a part of our heart; for when strife appears you will know that only **GOD's love will eliminate any type of fears**.

Keeping our faith is one of the greatest attributes of loving GOD – HE does not fail and through the Book of Job we can tell.

Life is full of consequences and choices; Trust in the Lord and use your voices to tell the world how **GREAT HE IS;** just wanting us to give HIM Praise every day is an awesome way to say **"THANK YOU JESUS" I LOVE YOU!!**

Amen

The Book of Job

THE LIGHT OF GOD

Darkness comes every **NIGHT** – isn't it great to awake and it is **LIGHT**; and the sunshine **BRIGHT** let us know JESUS is in our **SIGHT**.

Clouds can form very quickly, making it **DREARY;** we can sometimes become **WEARY**.

Clouds only last for a moment of time; when the sun comes out bright and warm we know deep within GOD is **NEAR;** there is absolutely nothing to **FEAR**.

When tears flow from hurt and **PAIN**, just remember Jesus' **CLAIM;** HE will not forsake us, thus keeping your faith **STRONG** will lead us to HIS **KINGDOM**.

GOD is the light of the world; keep HIS commandments, pray consistently and darkness will **DISAPPEAR;** again my sisters and brothers we must not have any **FEAR**.

Trust HIS words of wisdom, know HIS words are sincere; it's a total joy knowing we do not have to live with **STRESS** and that will allow us to pass one of GOD's special **TEST.**

We pray each day that the darkness in our lives will fade away; the light of GOD will control our **PATH** so that we can have a bright future that will **LAST**.

Amen!

Psalms 27:1

ANGER IS A TRICK

ANGER is an emotion that can put us in **DANGER**; we can control it by remembering GOD's **LOVE;** allowing HIM to strengthen us from **ABOVE**!

When in love with GOD's wisdom and doing our very best to abide by his **LAWS**; the evil one will interfere with our minds, tempt us with anger and that's a **FLAW.**

My sisters and brothers don't be **FOOLED;** have you noticed prisoners didn't have the **TOOL** to rebuke anger; thus they are incarcerated and now in **GRAVE DANGER**.

The bible was left of all to **READ**; believe me there is definitely a **NEED**; GOD has told us "Vengeance is Mine," HE will work it out for all to see in **HIS TIME!**

That awful emotion can lead to **PAIN** and bringing about anything **SANE**; saying words and doing things that we may **REGRET** do not solve problems only enhance the evil one's **THREAT**.

Resist that emotion it is nothing but a **TRAP**; we have too much at stake to fall for that **CRAP**.

DON'T BE TRICKED BY ANGER, let it go, give it to GOD; let HIM handle the vengeance from the start.
Amen!

Psalms 103:8

LOVING OUR CHILDREN

Teaching our children is a GOD given reaction, from birth to death we are their earthly protection.

It is a job like no other, for as parents it always makes us wonder, did we do our very best? GOD is the only judge of that awesome test.

There comes a time we must let go and pray our teachings will be imbedded in their souls, asking GOD to handle the rest with absolute control.

When GOD appointed us as parents HE gave us an awesome responsibility; to love and nurture our babies and teach them how to pray, surround them with love in the highest and most respectful way.

Teach our children HIS most sacred promises. Release them to HIM with the assurance HIS guidance will continue with the protection of his grace, during the turbulent times we know they will face!

Adulthood will surely come as time moves on and in that time period we must let go and know that we have done our very best, **NOW IT IS TIME TO LET GOD DO THE REST**!!

Amen!

Ephesians 6:1-4

"LISTENING TO GOD"

GOD is awesome in all HIS ways; HE created the universe in six days; when HIS creation came to us, the likeness of HIM was the beginning of trust.

Adam was the first man on earth, then HE created Eve to bear children and fill the world with mankind in paradise, what a great way to begin the human race.

We know through scripture they were told what to do; they were given instructions on how to live and should have known it was true.

LISTENING TO GOD IS A MUST; if peace is your desire in this world today then trusts what HE says and you will be amazed with how good life can be by putting HIM first always.

Action must follow for HIS words to be strong and not hollow; the Bible tells us over and over again, faith without works is definitely dead; **FOLLOW HIS INSTRUCTIONS AND YOU WILL BE LEAD.**

HE talks to us all in HIS special way, that's why it's so important that we **continuously pray**.

Amen!

James 2:20

WHAT'S GOING ON?

I'll tell you what's **GOING** on; evil is taking the weak, but not the **STRONG.**

Watch the evening news and see the devastation **GOING ON**, I say to you, stayed prayed up and let us all strive for GOD'S Kingdom ready to see Jesus on the **THRONE.**

Life is nothing but a test for **MANKIND**, materialistic things are a fool's fine **LINE**; no one to impress on this earth, strive for heaven, doing what **IS RIGHT** is what GOD demands during our **FIGHT.**

When we see evil in that horrible **FORMATION**, constantly praising the LORD should become our 1st **CONCENTRATION.**

Put on your **ARMOR OF FAITH** and keep it strapped tightly to your **SOUL,** and rest assured GOD has the undeniable **CONTROL.**

Amen!

1 Timothy 4:1-3
2 Timothy 3:1-6

THE DIFFERENT SEASONS

Leaves turn red, yellow, brown and green depending on the season that we are in; the weather is warm, hot, cool, and cold is a clear indication that season's **CHANGE** – giving GOD total authority in the grandest **RANGE**.

Man has no control of the color of leaves that changes on the **TREES,** nor has he control of the weather and sometime the weatherman cannot foresee what GOD Almighty has in store for you and **ME**.

Those are changes that affect human mankind and it should tell us that GOD has the control all the time; man cannot do anything about the season nor time because it is only GOD's **POWER** and things can change within the **HOUR!**

The birds fly as high as they want, no worry of food, water or evil as they envelope the **EARTH** – GOD takes care of them from their **BIRTH**.

When the snow falls from the sky, whom do you think brings it about and stops it without a thought? Certainly not man, he has **NO POWER**; God Almighty is our strength and our **TOWER**.

Spring time comes and flowers began to **BLOOM**, do you think man can make that happen, even though he has gone to the **MOON**?

Winter, spring, summer and fall, all part of GOD's creation let us know we are living on **HIS EARTH;** we must give HIM continuous praise by obeying **HIS LAWS** and following instructions **HE LEFT FOR ALL**.

Amen

Acts 1:7

LIFE IS BEAUTIFUL

When we see the birds and the **BEES** and look in awe at the beautiful **TREES**, we can see GOD's beauty in all **DEGREES**.

When we smile at strangers passing by and say have a blessed good **DAY**, when it comes from the heart it's easy to **SAY.**

When the sky is blue on a cloudless **DAY** and we feel GOD at work in his special **WAY**, you know deep within HE is **THERE** and HIS words are so very easy to **BEAR**.

When we lay down to sleep every **NIGHT**, there is a peace that envelops our spirits – It's GOD's love and that makes everything all **RIGHT**.

And, when we awake and happy to **PRAY,** it gives GOD delight in every **WAY**.

Yes, life is beautiful when you love GOD, trusting in HIS words and thanking HIM **CONSTANTLY,** we will see the special gifts HE has bestowed upon us **ABUNDANTLY.**

Amen

Genesis 2:8,9

AMAZING GRACE

Yes, GOD'S **GRACE** is amazing when we feel HIS spirit at work, for HIS business is uplifting us as we run life's **RACE**.

When obstacles' occur, HE is always there with HIS wings protecting us, then we can rest assured we will not go **ASTRAY**, but we must remember to continuously **PRAY**.

Powerful are HIS promises and we should know they are **TRUE**, for the bible tells us through and **THROUGH**.

HIS grace is amazing because HE will forgive us of our **SINS**, and put us on a righteous path to begin anew, but we are not to continue that **SIN**, or we will be left out in the **END**.

HE wants us to trust HIS words and put them into **ACTION** every day; and in doing so we will have HIS grand **PROTECTION**.

Amazing is our LORD for HE is **REAL**, from deep in your spirit you can **FEEL** HIS presence within, keep it close at all **TIMES** and you will illuminate like the beautiful warm bright **SUNSHINE**.

Amen!!

2 John 1:3
2 Peter 3:18

WHEN TIMES ARE TOUGH

We hear this phrase quite often these **DAYS**; they say "TIMES ARE TOUGH" in all different kind of **WAYS**.

I say never too tough for the LORD to handle – release it to HIM and follow HIS **DIRECTION** is the most efficient way for a true **CORRECTION**.

There is nothing that GOD cannot **DO;** but you must give it to HIM and know it is **TRUE**.

Say you have faith and continue to worry, it just doesn't **MIX!!!** When you leave it to HIM and be patient, rest assured HE will provide a real **FIX**.

Yes, it's true times are **TOUGH** and it can become extremely **ROUGH;** when your FAITH takes over all **WORRY**, that's the exact time GOD will change that negative **STORY**.

So I say, trust the LORD with all your heart, mind and **SOUL**; then you will see who has undeniable **CONTROL!!**

Amen

Psalms 37:2-7

WE ARE SPECIAL

Our creation is in the likeness of GOD, what a privilege it is to represent HIM, for HE is great in all that HE **DOES;** HE make no mistakes and we should know that is **TRUE**.

HE gives us the freedom of **CHOICE,** so make your decisions wisely by representing HIM, one of the ways is with your **VOICE**

There is no **SHAME** when calling out HIS **NAME**; when we do we claim HIS awesome glory and **FAME**

HE made no mistakes when HE created us in all HIS **GLORY**, there is something HE wants from us, **PUT HIM FIRST THAT IS HIS STORY**.

HE is the highest and the **BEST** the world has ever known; never forget that during your earthly **TEST**.

Get on your knees praying morning, noon and night, thanking HIM; Praising HIM that your needs are being met; knowing HE will not leave you in times of **TROUBLE;** we are special, **WHAT AN AWESOME WONDER.**

Amen

Genesis 1:26-31

GOD IS NEAR

We've all been in situations that gave us have a tingle of **FEAR**; calling out GOD'S name immediately you know HE is **NEAR!**

We've all experienced a **VOICE** within; when it's a **CHOICE** we have to make in a matter of seconds, GOD will tell us what to do **NEXT**, just listen and put it into action, the key is don't become **VEXTED**.

For we cannot see HIM, but HIS spirit is **STRONG**; do the right thing and resist doing anything **WRONG**, because our ultimate goal is striving for HIS THRONE.

When death prevails with our family and **FRIENDS**, we should rejoice because the spirit within us will never **END**.

Look forward to the day we will see them again, when we have followed GOD's plan; rest assure united we will be again.

For John 14: 1-3 tell us **"LET OUR HEARTS NOT BE TROUBLED, HE HAS PREPARED A PLACE FOR US AND HE WILL COME AND RECEIVE US IN HIS FATHER'S HOUSE"!** Our job now is to follow GOD's **WILL** and make it to HIS mansions where our souls will rest in peace where it will be a **THRILL** to be with JESUS.

Amen.

John 14:1-3

THE GOALS

The goals in life should be sturdy and **BOLD**, for GOD gives us freedom of will; surely, the first goal is to give **GOD ALMIGHTY CONTROL**. When we trust and believe in HIM, HE lifts us up; suffer not my children is a message for **US**!

The next goal should always be putting HIM **FIRST,** never having to worry about hunger or **THIRST**; for the 23rd Psalms tell us loud and **CLEAR**, the LORD is my Shepherd there is nothing to **FEAR**.

It is so obvious HE is our **PROTECTION**, that's why it's so important to have a strong **CONNECTION** with our FATHER in HEAVEN.

HE will bring us through all trials and tribulations, and keep us **STRONG** when things go **WRONG**; HE can make it **RIGHT**, just believe it, and sometimes it can turn around **OVERNIGHT**.

We all have experienced negative **THINGS**, and in our spirit we must give it to our **KING;** HIS guidance is strong and **STRAIGHT**, regardless of what we go through we should never **HATE**.

The goal of all times is to love and trust our **HEAVENLY FATHER**, for when we do nothing else really **MATTERS**.

Amen

Psalms 23

GETTING OUR ATTENTION

When we see tornadoes destroying our **LAND**, there is a message for all humans once **AGAIN**!

We see floods filling our **HOMES** and sinkholes swallowing up everything that we **OWN.** We should know GOD doesn't do this; HE allows the evil one to see to whom we **BELONG;** during these times call out HIS name loud and **STRONG.**

Murder and **MAIM** is on the rampage; it makes me wonder how folks cannot or will not call out HIS **NAME**; for GOD's protection we should all **CLAIM.**

The survivors on TV and not thanking HIM for being **SPARED**; it makes me wonder how they **PREPARED.**

GOD wants our glory and praise during the turbulent times that envelops the earth during the last days, we know the last days are **HERE** because the scriptures make it extremely **CLEAR.**

Hurricanes come to destroy with great gust of winds, we pray to be spared from hurt and **PAIN**; this is a way for the evil one to put us in dark **CHAINS.** GOD wants to know we believe in HIM and trust HIS holy words with actions and not fear; **GOD IS ALWAYS NEAR!!**

Amen

Matthew 24:6-7

REMEMBER THIS SONG

"JESUS LOVES THE LITTLE CHILDREN, ALL THE CHILDREN OF THE WORLD, THEY CAN BE YELLOW, BLACK OR WHITE, THEY ARE PRECIOUS IN HIS SITE, JESUS LOVE THE LITTLE CHILDREN OF THE WORLD."

Thus we come into the 21st century and see the injustices done to children; it let us know the evil one is raising havoc on the **YOUNG**, but **GOD'S WILL**, will be **DONE**.

When we experience the prejudices of today because the color of one's **SKIN**; we can only ask "GOD to forgive them of their **SIN**."

There are many things we cannot **UNDERSTAND**; one thing we know, evil is definitely in our **LAND;** yet evil will not withstand GOD's Almighty **HAND**.

When justice rain **DOWN** there is no way to get out of **TOWN**; because justice will find you wherever you are**, NEAR OR FAR**.

Keeping our spirit strong and **CLEAR**, we have to constantly know **GOD IS NEAR** and we must continuously pray and always rebuke **FEAR**.

Amen

John 13:35

BELIEVE IN HIS WORDS

The Bible is on earth for a definite **REASON;** it gives us instructions for every **SEASON;** it lets us know who we should praise each and every **DAY** to prevent our spirits from going **ASTRAY.**

HE left this Bible full of **INSTRUCTIONS;** showing us throughout the evil one is nothing but **DESTRUCTION.**

The bible gives us **NUMEROUS** stories in the old and new testaments, so that we may have a road map to HIS **GLORIES.**

Words are easy to say, putting them into **ACTION** will provide our souls with true **SATISFACTION.**

When we believe in HIS words and call out HIS **NAME,** whatever we encounter will never bring **SHAME.**

So believe in HIS words, trust in HIS holy **NAME** and life's victories you will be able to **CLAIM.**

Amen

Romans 9:33

NO NEED TO COMPLAIN

When we **COMPLAIN**, that negativism will put us in the devil's **CHAIN**. Thanking GOD by praising HIM for a new chance every **DAY**, shows our gratitude to our FATHER as we **PRAY**.

For every complaint there is lots of blessings; let me give you a few examples; thank GOD when you awake and have no **PAIN**, nor have you awaken in jail or in **CHAINS**.

Count your blessings for they are positive; another example is when your financial funds are low; thank HIM for what's getting ready to come because GOD can move mountains and part the sea (**Hallelujah**) **HE can do all things for you and me.**

Complaints shows ungratefulness; when we complain it does not bring about prosperity, only shame of what we have **NOT**, being grateful for all we have will brighten our spirits right on the **SPOT**.

Find good in all that surrounds us and more blessing will occur through a thankful **SOUL**; knowing deep in our hearts GOD really has the righteous **CONTROL**.

Stop the complaining for it does no good, count all your blessing and you will **SEE,** this is the place GOD want us to **BE**.

Amen!!

Romans 1:21
Ephesians 4

THIS STORY IS TRUE

Christ walked this earth with life and **LOVE,** sent from our Heavenly Father above.

HE brought a message for all mankind; **LOVE** one another, including our enemies; **LOVE** can heal diseases and cleanse the soul; **LOVE** has positive effects and is awesome and bold.

HIS lessons are true in this day and time; believe it by putting them into action during the most **TURBULENT TIMES** and our inner spirit will **TRULY SHINE**.

JESUS told them there was only one **TRUE KING**, and this King was not on earth; unbelievers nailed HIM to a cross; I guess to show JESUS who was the boss.

Died HE did on that cross and **ASKED GOD TO FORGIVE THEM OF THEIR SINS;** it shows us how JESUS loved mankind and gave HIS life so that we could have a chance to shine; the SON OF GOD died for our sins and that is **REALLY TRUE**.

GOD raised HIM from the dead, **THUS WAS BORN TRUE BELIEVERS INSTEAD** – and today they are spreading HIS messages all over the land.

The lessons HE taught are still true today, so I say my sisters and brothers, **FOLLOW HIS WORDS OF WISDOM WITHOUT DELAY!!!**

Amen

Hebrews 12:2

SPIRITUALITY FIRST NOT MATERIALIST THINGS

There is nothing materialist on this earth that can replace GOD's truth and love for us since before our birth.

We cannot buy love, peace, respect or happiness; it comes from within and how we treat strangers, family and friends.

Big cars, fine homes, beautiful clothes and jewelry have some of us thinking we've got it going on; those things will not assist us in making it to **GOD'S THRONE.**

The **LORD gives and the LORD takes away**; keep your spirits right, looking for GOD's guidance as we continuously **PRAY FOR HIS PROTECTION EACH SECOND OF EVERY DAY.**

Don't get caught up in praising stuff, that's when GOD says, "that's enough" in the blink of an eye it can disappear; **ONLY DISOBEYING GOD'S COMMANDMENTS WE SHOULD ALL FEAR.**

GOD wants our praise and to do the right thing and in doing that first we will have *EVERYTHING!!*

Amen

Mark 8:36

PROTECT YOUR THOUGHTS

Protect your minds with goodness and gratefulness every second of the day; scriptures tell us we should **CONTINUOUSLY PRAY**.

The evil one wants our soul and mind; but when we pray to *ALMIGHTY GOD* it sets the evil one behind.

When negative thoughts cross our minds, shout out **GOD'S NAME**; peace will replace that ugly game the devil plays; get on your knees and pray; pray for your thoughts to be of **PEACE, LOVE AND GRACE** as we move on with life running this crucial race.

GOD loves us unconditionally, that's why it is so important to pray continuously in all we do; **THIS IS A GREAT THING FOR ME AND YOU!!!**

When thinking of **GOD'S LOVE AND GRACE** and allowing it to consume our minds; we will find peace deep within and that takes our minds off sin, the sin that helps the evil one win!!!

Watch your thoughts every second of every day and know *GOD ALMIGHTY WILL PROTECT US IN EVERY WAY!!*

Amen

John 15:9-17

THE HOLIDAY SEASON

Christmas has become so commercialized that people forget the true reason for this season.

Giving gifts from our heart is the key to loving GOD; this should be throughout the year and especially during the holiday season.

Give to those who don't suspect you're giving to get something back; because that will defeat the true reason for this season.

THINK ABOUT THIS:
Christmas Day children are in the hospital for illnesses and/or mishaps and many have to stay on this special day.

Wrap your gifts for these children with GOD'S love; HE is paying attention from high above.

Go to the hospitals on this special day; while giving gifts believe and pray the gifts you are giving will brighten a child's day.

Amen

James 1:17

GOD'S POWER

GOD'S power is strong, bold, and awesome; He can move mountains and part the sea, one thing HE wants is for us to believe.

We've all experienced HIS power and glory and guaranteed each one of us have a story; been in situations that we had no clue of what to do, but you know and I know **GOD CAME THROUGH**.

We've seen HIS healing hands and protection from evil, we've also seen HIS wrath for unbelievers; Christians know that it is true; GOD will lead and guide us through and through.

HIS love for us is undeniable, HIS mercy and grace is shown in every way, that's why it's so important that **WE CONTINUOUSLY PRAY**.

KEEP YOUR ARMOR OF FAITH STRAPPED ON TIGHT, for the fight between good and evil is going on morning, noon and night.

The only way to win this serious war is to know GOD is by our side and all **HIS LAWS WE MUST ABIDE**!

Amen

2ⁿᵈ Timothy 1:7

GENUINE LOVE

This type of love began from above – when we were created it was true Love from our Heavenly Father smiling down on HIS greatest creation from above.

Through GOD'S SON HE showed how much HE love us; sent HIS SON to die for our sins; an awesome sacrifice and all mankind should feel deep within.

HE told us to love one another and give us examples in the scriptures over and over again.

Genuine love never hurts or maim, it never leads us to be ashamed; when HE told us to love our enemies, HE knew how difficult that would be, but left us scriptures to know that in doing so we would be eternally set free.

When HE told us **"Vengeance Is Mine",** it took the burden off of us. Turn that ugly emotion of anger into a love that will keep us in HIS righteous time line.

That love is so great, that it will not allow for us to hate; if we do it will undermine our fate.

True love forgives deep within; all of us has to constantly rebuke sin. No other emotion of love can come close; GOD has shown us **HE LOVES US THE MOST.**

Amen

Deuteronomy 32:35

GOOD FRUITS OF THE SPIRIT

Bishop Gresham taught us the goodness of GOD, pointing out the good fruits appointed by the LORD; they are **love, peace, kindness, forgiveness, joyfulness** and **faith**; it's written in the scriptures for all to receive; don't give in to the evil one and be deceived.

These fruits are fulfilling our **SPIRITUAL NEEDS**, helping us with despair and strife; thus we can live a prosperous and joyous life.

Spiritual fruits are nourished and grown each day with faith of the **LORD'S** words and be assured HE want us to partake.

The scriptures tell us over and over again how good life can be, just putting **OUR FAITH** in all HIS words. We must not allow anything to disturb us on this earth, for it is our LORD we must always trust.

So I say, enjoy the good fruits of life. Watch and see, the strife of everyday life will be diminished as we continue on this earth praising the LORD and **ENJOYING THE GOOD FRUITS OF LIFE**.

Amen

Galatians 5:22

MIND BOGGLING

Remember the slang, "Blow your mind"? Well, GOD's amazing grace and HIS works will blow your mind, because **HE IS ALWAYS ON TIME**.

HE gives us instructions each and every day, and when following through it's easy to say, **"GOD IS GOOD IN HIS AWESOME AND RIGHTEOUS WAY."**

When giving HIM all our problems we have no worries, because HE will work it out in **HIS TIME PERIOD!**

Yes my sisters and brothers, **IT IS MIND BOGGLING HOW GOD CAN WORK IT OUT,** we know it's HIM; we do not have the capacity nor could we have thought how simple and direct **HE** works all things out.

GIVE IT TO HIM with a full understanding, **GOD CAN WORK IT OUT**; the struggle will be eliminated HIS blessings are mighty and bold, because in the scriptures it has been foretold.

Amen

Psalms 91:2

WAKE UP PEOPLE

Wake up with GOD's words on your mind;
    Thanking HIM continuously;
        Put HIS words into action all the time;

For we are living in the last days before CHRIST is to appear;
    Those who worship the true living GOD have nothing to fear;
        GOD has a book of life where all of our names will appear.

HE left the Bible for all mankind to read and understand;
    It's just a matter of time when the answers are revealed;
        Waiting on HIS answers are such a fantastic thrill.

Good and evil will be separated;
    Peace on earth will be for a thousand years;
        HE promises there will be no more tears.

Wake up people with your armor of peace, protection and grace;
    Look forward to peace on earth that we all need to embrace.

Amen

Isiah 24:8

WHEN BIRDS SING

Early in the mornings when the birds sing, they are giving praise to our **AWESOME KING;** their melody is strong with power and grace, thanking GOD for protection in all they will face.

They fly so beautifully without stress -- knowing unconditionally GOD created them with the **BEAUTY THEY POSSESS**.

When we hear and see the beauty of the birds, we should immediately be reminded of GOD's love for us; **WE ARE HIS GREATEST CREATION.** Therefore, we should **ALWAYS PRAISE HIM WITHOUT HESITATION.**

Psalms 23 tell us in the first verse, "The Lord is my Shepherd, I shall not want", that's easy to understand; HE will take care of us because **HE HOLDS US IN HIS HOLY HANDS.**

The birds understand and live that verse every day; so when you hear them sing, just know they are giving thanksgiving and prayers to our **ALMIGHTY HEAVENLY KING.**

Amen

Psalms 23

IMPOSSIBLE? NO!!

Nothing is impossible with the faith of GOD; **BELIEF AND TRUST IS A MUST!** We all know what HE told NOAH to do; NOAH followed GOD's instructions; only GOD knew of the upcoming destruction!

Ask no questions when given directions and instructions from GOD; the future will tell you why it was extremely important **TO FOLLOW HIS DIRECTIONS FROM YOUR HEART.**

HE tells us through the scripture, **"A MUSTARD SEED OF FAITH WILL DO";** throughout centuries we know it is true.

Scientist cannot prove the workings of faith, but our experiences show faith is real; and as it works, we know **HOW GOOD GOD IS!**

IMPOSSIBLE? NO!! WITH GOD ALL THINGS ARE POSSIBLE! HE has power stronger than we can comprehend; HE answers our prayers in HIS time and HIS way, in many cases it's without delay.

NOTHING IS IMPOSSIBLE WHEN IT COMES TO GOD; YOU MUST KNOW THAT AND BELIEVE IT DEEP WITHIN YOUR HEART!!!

Amen

Matthew 17:20
Philippians 4:13

DO NOT GO BACKWARDS

Marching forward is the way to go; slipping backwards will slow us from the path GOD wants us to know.

The spiritual fight goes on day and night; we all need to walk in GOD's light. Keep your mind and spirit on doing what is right.

Evil hates the beauty of CHRIST and hates us even more for believing in HIS life. That's the darkness that wants to take us backwards.

Recognizing evil's delight, stop in your tracks and take a deep breath; moving forward with GOD and HIS words constantly will bring us **SPIRITUAL WEALTH**.

GOD's love will elevate us forward toward HIS light, thus making our future extremely bright.

STRENGTHEN YOUR FAITH each and every day; keep moving forward and let nothing cause a delay!

Amen

Proverbs 14:14
Matthew 5:14-16

FAITH IN ACTION

When horrible obstacles occur and try to scare the wits out of us; faith says to be cool. You don't have to react in a frightened way; **GOD IS WITH YOU AND THAT'S A FACT**!

When faith kicks in and inner peace occurs, that's when you know GOD can handle anything; giving our problems is to HIM is acknowledging that **HE IS THE UNDENIABLE KING**.

GOD is our witness through our highs and lows; HE sees and knows all things deep within. HE knows how many hairs are on our heads and always provide us with our daily bread.

Understand negative things will happen; GOD has a way of turning those things around, with our faith we will be the ones that **GOD CROWNS**.

HIS love is like a parent's love, it's strong, it's protective and it's secure. Obey HIM we must and when we do so with **TOTAL TRUST IN GOD AND HIS WORDS,** then we will not be frightened or disturbed.

So I say in this poem, **KEEP YOUR FAITH IN GOD SOLID AND STRONG**, so we all can meet again in GOD's Kingdom, as we enjoy **SITTING WITH HIM ON HIS ALMIGHTY THRONE**!

Amen

Ephesians 3:17

VIOLENCE IS RUNNING WILD

Turn on the news and we all can see violence is throughout the entire world; why are things getting so bad? People are being deceived by the evil one in our land; having no knowledge of truth as **GOD ALMIGHTY PLANNED.**

Murder and maim has become a very sick game; it is one of the ways the devil claims destruction; his negative spirit entering mankind and fooling them into thinking this nonsense is justified.

There is a counter to the negativity going on in our land; it is the protection of GOD having us, protecting us and keeping us in HIS hands as evil surrounds us wanting to take command.

BELIEVE IN GOD WITH ALL YOUR HEART, MIND AND SOUL; and I guarantee you the evil one cannot take control.

JESUS was tested on this very same earth; died for our sins so that we could live on; rebuke the evil one and stay strong.

Remember GOD's love for us every second of each day; it cannot be emphasized enough how **IMPORTANT IT IS TO CONTINUOUSLY PRAY**.

Amen

James 4:7

THIS NEW YEAR

We thank our Heavenly Father to see another year; HE tells us following HIS words we have nothing to fear!

HE continuously shows us how to put our trust in HIS SON; when we do we have already won.

Know Lucifer's spirit is on the earth; his job is to surround us with obstacles, evilness and hate; his ugly spirit makes that clear, leaving people in despair and having anxiety of fear.

We all should know that when our spirits are with GOD, keeping HIS words deep in our hearts; doing the right things GOD ask of us and we should never depart.

Be grateful for a true living GOD; HE let us see another year; another new year to give praise and thank HIM from our hearts; remember my sisters and brothers HE is real and we should all praise HIM with exuberance and not fear!

Amen

Psalms 43:4

HOLD ON!

HOLD ON to GOD'S words, know they are true; HE only wants what is good for those who believe in HIM, so they can become brand new.

HOLD ON as each day begins anew; study GOD'S words and knowledge will be given to you.

HOLD ON to GOD'S directions and instructions; it will be a road map to peaceful transactions.

HOLD ON to righteousness day in and day out; for righteousness will guide your spirits morning, noon and night.

HOLD ON to your faith in GOD; faith is the key to Jesus' heart; when things get out of whack know GOD is with you, HE will protect, that is a true fact!

HOLD ON to your peace which comes from deep within your soul; never give in to evil or sin and never let it take control.

HOLD ON to good dreams GOD has given for your life; although you will run into difficulties making those dreams a reality; never give up for GOD will show you the finish line HE has established, it will be right on time!

Amen

Psalms 44:7-8

TAKE OFF THE BLINDERS

We all know the song, **"I WAS BLIND, BUT NOW I SEE"**, it means at one time we were blind, but THANK GOD the blinders were removed and now we can see, **HALLELUJAH FOR YOU AND ME.**

The truth will always prevail; when the blinders come off we can see the difference in right and wrong and heaven and hell.

Blinds keep the **(SUN)** out and the **(SON)** wants us to see the light and to understand we are all in a serious spiritual fight; the war is who gets our soul; and we only have control!

GOD ALMIGHTY created us for HIM; and the evil one wants us for himself; want to know who will win? GOD will win, but what side will we be on before the fight ends? Take off the blinders and look deep within; then and only then can we make changes before this time period ends.

Once the blinders have been removed, it is easier to see; the choices we make are very clear; no standing on the fence as time moves on; it's either godly right or evil wrong; make the right choice and be strong!

Pray for your blinders to be removed permanently; ask GOD to show you HIS direction toward HIS KINGDOM; pray that you can see clearly each and every day; keep your heart, soul and mind right as you continuously pray!

Amen

2 Corinthians 4:4

RECOGNIZING MIRACLES

Waking up is a miracle today;
Waking up with a sound mind;
Waking up with protection from the elements;
Waking up and standing up;
Waking up and walking are miracles we should never take for granted; GOD is
the reason miracles occur; **Thank HIM!**

Talking with clarity and sense;
Talking and others understand you;
Talking about GOD and HIS miracles, testifying;
Talking the truth of your experience;
Talking truth for understanding;
Talking should never be taken for granted;
GOD is the reason miracles occur; **Thank HIM!**

Eating breakfast is a miracle;
Eating lunch is a miracle;
Eating dinner is a miracle;
Eating snacks are a miracle;
Eating with loved ones is a miracle that we should never take for granted;
GOD is the reason miracles occur; **Thank HIM!**

Parents who love us are a miracle;
Parents who teach us right from wrong are a miracle
Parents who nurture us are a miracle;
Parents who provide our needs are a miracle;
Parents who are good and LOVE GOD are a miracle that we should never take for granted;
GOD is the reason miracles occur, **Thank HIM!**

John 11:39-45

EXPERENCING GRACE

GRACE is given to humans for their regeneration and sanctification; this comes from our *CREATOR* who loves us more than words can express; grace is given to those who do what is right and give their very best.

GRACE is a controlled, polite and a pleasant way of behaving; a special kindness coming from GOD; rebuke all sin and never depart.

GRACE is approval, mercy and pardon; it comes from GOD it should be known and imbedded in our spirits and deep in our hearts.

GRACE is a gift from GOD; through faith grace is given; keep your faith strong as can be for GOD ALMIGHTY certainly loves you and me.

GRACE is given to the humbled indeed; resist the spirit of boastfulness and pride; with GOD ALMIGHTY no one can hide.

GROW IN GRACE; it's another example of how to run this spiritual race; resist doing all things that are wrong; with GOD'S grace transforming us with a walkway to HIS throne.

Amen

Ephesians 2:5-8
1 Peter 5:5

STAND UP

STAND UP with your heads held high; GOD ALMIGHTY is great and will not be denied; the wisdom HE possess is in the scriptures for all to read; believe, receive, then your life with be better indeed.

STAND UP to the evils of the world; from your hearts do what is right, and fight your sinful ways morning, noon and night.

STAND UP and receive GOD'S love; rejoice and be happy deep in your souls, letting our HEAVENLY FATHER take total control.

STAND UP for those that seek the truth; teach them and help them receive faith; and you will be given GOD'S special grace.

STAND UP for GOD'S wisdom; put it all into action, when we do our souls will receive a great satisfaction.

STAND UP for the poor and disgruntled; showing them how to survive with GOD'S protection, maintaining HIS teachings by being humble.

STAND UP for what is right; it is certainly a fight in this spiritual war that is going on; we've been promised by GOD ALMIGHTY to rebuke sin so that we may see our LORD once again.

This poem shall end with this; **"STAND UP FOR JESUS CHRIST"** always follow HIS will by doing what is right and is pleasing in HIS sight; then you shall have HIS ALMIGHTY protection morning, noon and night.

Amen

Revelation 6:17

FORGIVENESS

When Christ died for our sins HIS last words were **"FATHER FORGIVE THEM, FOR THEY KNOW NOT WHAT THEY DO"**.

If HE can ask forgiveness for nailing HIM to the cross; then our forgiveness of others should never be lost.

GOD WILL FORGIVE US OF OUR SINS; when we have been mistreated by family and friends; we must pray for them and forgive them for us to win.

It's a difficult thing to do; but loving GOD and forgiving is the righteous thing for us too!

For GOD to forgive us of our wrongs we must forgive others, thus is a way to make it to GOD'S throne. Forgiving is a mindset, guaranteed we will never regret.

Forgiveness must come from a spiritual mind and we should practice it all the time; holding grudges is definitely a sin and will bring us down in the end.

Let us all ask for forgiveness from our LORD; forgive those who caused us pain; when we forgive those whom have wronged us, we will be free of a negative heart for **GOD HAS PROMISED US A GREAT REWARD**.

Amen

Matthew 6:12, 14-15

PRAYER IN SCHOOLS

It has become frequent these days; children with guns in the schools; they have not been taught about GOD's special tools or HIS awesome rules.

Children are raising themselves without guidance anywhere; there is anger and rage deep within them; never been taught about GOD's protection; so they succumb to an evil reaction.

TO THE CHILDREN READING THIS POEM; know GOD is real and HIS protection strong; **PRAY YOU MUST WHEN THINGS GO WRONG**!

Although prayer has been taken out of schools; you can always pray and that is your greatest tool!

Vengeance is not the way to go; loving GOD is what you must to show; when others provoke yourself control, remember GOD'S love, stand up for HIM and be bold;

Know and understand evil is surrounding us in our land; fight with love and prayer and GOD ALMIGHTY with handle it from there.

Amen

Ephesians 1:19
Psalms 34:4

GOD'S POWER

GOD'S power is strong, bold, and awesome; HE can move mountains and part the sea, one thing HE wants is for us to believe.

We've all experienced HIS power and glory, guaranteed each one of us have a story; been in situations we had no clue of what to do, when we prayed GOD came through.

We've seen HIS healing hands and protection from evil; we've also seen HIS wrath for unbelievers; Christians know it's true; GOD will lead and guide us through and through.

HIS love for us is undeniable, HIS mercy and grace is shown in every way, that's why it's so important that we continuously pray.

Keep your armor of faith strapped on tight, for the fight between good and evil is going on day and night.

The only way to win this spiritual war is to know **GOD IS BY OUR SIDE AND ALL HIS LAWS WE MUST ABIDE.**

Amen

Matthew 28:18

GENUINE LOVE

When we were created it was true Love from our Heavenly Father smiling down on HIS greatest creation from above.

Through HIS SON HE showed how much HE loves us; sent HIS SON to die for our sins, what a sacrifice for mankind and we should feel it deep within.

GOD told us to love one another and gives us examples in the scriptures over and over again; genuine love is from the heart and one cannot pretend.

Love never hurts or maims, it never leads us to be shame; when HE told us to love our enemies, HE knew how difficult that would be, left us scriptures to know in doing so we could be free.

When HE told us "vengeance is mine", it took the burden off us to relinquish that emotion into a love that will keep us in HIS righteous time line.

That love is so great, it will not allow for us to hate; for if we do, it will undermine our spiritual fate.

This type of love forgives deep within, know that all of us have the potential to sin; no other emotion can come close, **BECAUSE GOD HAS SHOWN US HE LOVES US MOST.**

Amen

John 15:9-13

REPROBATED MIND!

Head strong and a heart that is wrong; a reprobated mind will not make it to God's throne.

Learning the scriptures and not putting them in action; making a mockery out of the truth; gaining nothing but heart ache and pain and that is all that will remain.

That type of spirit is easy to notice; always complaining and raising hell is a sure way we all can tell.

That mind is confrontational and negative in all communication; when Christians try to help it leaves us weak and tired because we know they are trapped; trapped in an evil pattern they will never make it to heaven.

I've come to the conclusion that these changes must come from deep within their spirits; pray we must for them to learn before it's too late and ask GOD ALMIGHTY to help them with their spiritual fate.

NOW I SAY TO THE REPROBATED SPIRIT, YOU ARE MISSING OUT ON A VERY IMPORTANT DAY; WHEN GOD'S JUDGMENT COME WHAT WILL YOU SAY?

Amen

1 Timothy 6:4-5

GET READY!

GET READY Sisters and Brothers for the challenges we all will face, as we live, work and play.

GET READY because the evil one wants our soul; study GOD's words and put them into action will help us through with great satisfaction.

GET READY because GOD has given us direct instructions on how to have faith in HIS holy words; remember them and do not become disturbed.

GET READY for trials and tribulations; implement GOD'S commandments and HIS directions; beware of evil in your mist; stand up for what is right never using your fist.

GET READY for stumbles and tumbles; during this time period stay sincere and humble.

GET READY to obey GOD'S will; keep your spirits right; know that we are all in a spiritual fight.

GET READY for good rewards as we practice GOD'S commandments; keeping our souls in line; **KNOW THAT GOD ALMIGHTY IS ALWAYS RIGHT ON TIME!**

Amen

Psalms 4:4-5

WHAT IS IT ALL ABOUT?

What is it all about? **PRAISING GOD** when things are good, bad, happy or sad makes HIM happy about HIS plans.

What is it all about? Waking up every day **PRAISING THE LORD** as we work and play gives GOD delight in every way.

What is it all about? Knowing whatever we should face, **GOD IS HOLDING US UP WITH HIS GRACE.**

What is it all about? **GOING TO GOD FOR ALL OUR NEEDS** do not put your trust in man; when you do disappointment will prevail; putting your total faith in GOD and know HE never fails!

What is it all about? **OBEYING GOD'S COMMANDMENTS**; helping others in need is what HE asks; loving one another without a mask.

IT'S ALL ABOUT GOD ALMIGHTY, *THE ALPHA AND THE OMEGA*; THE FIRST AND THE LAST; PUTTING HIM FIRST MUST BE OUR NUMBER ONE THOUGHT; CANNOT BE SOLD OR BOUGHT; PUT YOUR TOTAL TRUST IN HIM – THAT'S WHAT IT'S ALL ABOUT!!!

Amen

Revelation 1:11

TRIALS AND TRIBULATIONS

Know that trials and tribulations are a part of life; how we deal with them can enhance or diminish strife in our everyday life.

Go through them with a grateful heart; ask GOD to show you how to overcome this challenging part; HE will and it won't be hard.

You may ask, how do I be grateful when it appears my life is falling apart? Know that GOD is in the miracle making business; HIS promises are true; HIS truth never departs.

Strong faith in GOD and knowing HE can and will work it out; should make us happy without any doubt.

Remember the trial that JOB went through? He lost everything he owned and through the scriptures it was true; JOB was not happy about the challenges he faced; his loved continued for GOD even after his wife walked out without a trace.

GOD knew that JOB was a faithful servant and let him be tested by the evil one; JOB passed the test with heartache and pain; GOD ALMIGHTY tripled his desires once again.

Be thankful for trials and tribulations in life; go through them without stress or strife; your rewards will be greater than one can imagine in your life!!

Amen

Book of Job

STAYING POWER!

STAYING in the LORD morning, noon and night will give us staying power when the evil one challenges our life.

STAYING with our FATHER through all obstacles will make life easier to bear when our tribulations don't seem fair.

STAYING with studying the scriptures and learning GOD's words can only enhance our knowledge; something that is not taught in college.

STAYING deep in the faith and grace of GOD brings about a peace that we should never want to depart.

STAYING power is every second of the day, for you and I both know the evil one wants us to stumble and never pray.

STAYING with the righteous spirit of GOD; life will be happier before our bodies go back to the earth; it's where we came from birth.

STAYING in the truth of right and wrong; choosing the right way will ultimately lead us to GOD's ALMIGHTY throne.

STAYING with GOD's words each and every day; make it a habit to continuously pray.

STAYING PURE IN YOUR HEART; FOR THEY SHALL SEE GOD!

Amen.

Matthew 5:3-11

HAPPY IS A MAN

HAPPY is a man with GOD's words always in HIS plans.

HAPPY is a man that puts GOD first; for GOD's knowledge he has a unquenchable thirst.

HAPPY is a man who prays constantly; that man knows GOD's great qualities.

HAPPY is a man who praises GOD in all he does; for that man knows GOD's words are entirely true and no exemptions for me and you.

HAPPY is a man who treats others right; he refuses to get angry and definitely will not fight.

HAPPY is a man who has GOD's grace; he never worries about the challenges he will face.

HAPPY is a man who loves deeply; HE understands the love of GOD; and that man will never depart.

HAPPY is a man who gives to others; he is the type of man that makes others wonder.

HAPPY is a man that knows GOD's words; that man will trust and love our LORD without a doubt; that man will know how to handle life's curves and he never pouts!!

Amen

Psalms 144:15

"A GREAT BATTLE"

The battle between good and evil is in full force; both want our bodies, minds, spirits and souls; **THIS BATTLE IS FIERCE AND BOLD!**

GOD does not force us to love and obey; HE gives us free will to choose the road we will take. **IT'S OUR CHOICE, WHICH CHOICE WILL WE MAKE?**

The evil one wants to be praised; wants control in all the negative ways; the battle pursues all mankind; it's here right now in our time.

This battle affects our minds, bodies and soul; it is up to us not to let the evil one take control.

Brothers and Sisters you know it is true; this battle is being fought for me and you; GOD deserves us all; go to HIM with the highest of trust, keeping HIM in your heart you must!

We know GOD ALMIGHTY will win in the end; understand in this battle we all are pawns; **THE RIGHT SIDE IS GOD'S MERCY, LOVE AND GRACE WILL WIN THIS BATTLE THAT WE ALL FACE**.

Amen.

2 Timothy 2:3-4

ATTENTION TO GOD

GOD wants our attention in all we do; HE is the reason Jesus Christ died for me and you!

HE deserves our prayers every day; HE is the Grand master and does not want HIS children to stray.

When the world seems so cruel and mean; only GOD's power can keep us beneath HIS wings.

All HE asks is to acknowledge HIM in everything we do; over and over again HE has shown us HE will come through.

GOD is our refuge and our strength to a peaceful existence on this earth when we sincerely repent; sin no more is what HE wants.

HE gets our attention with the mountains we must climb; having total faith in GOD, HE will never leave us behind.

GOD wants our love for HIM to be first; HE is not a GOD that leaves HIS people in want when we thirst.

HIS attention is captivating; waking up in the mornings there is no speculating; HE wants us to pronounce HIS name loud and keep it circulating.

GIVE GOD THE ATTENTION THAT HE SO RICHLY DESERVES; STOP COMPLAINING; BE GRATEFUL, FOR ALL THAT HE DOES COMES FROM THE HEAVENS ABOVE.

Amen

Psalm 40:10, 16

THE END WILL COME

GOD is so awesome in all HIS ways; HE knows how many days we have on this earth; HE gives none of us a clue; GOD has known before our birth.

We all have experienced death with family and friends; without a doubt we know our lives will end.

Rejoice when one leaves this earthly place; that emotion is stymied knowing on earth we will never again see their face; as we continue to live on and run life's race.

Time on earth is temporary -- our bodies are temporary too; we are on borrowed time, that's for everyone, all of us know it's true; our souls live on; we should concentrate on reaching GOD ALMIGHTY'S throne.

Eternal life is what we must strive for; eternal never ending; the good part is meeting those who obeyed GOD's commandments; it will be a new day, a new beginning.

Meeting them at GOD's footstool; we can't do that if we continue to be fooled by the evil one that will never be at the footstool of CHRIST; to get there we must not be fooled!

Amen

John 5:24

OPEN UP!

OPEN UP sisters and brothers to the knowledge of GOD; once you get it, you should never depart.

OPEN UP to the truth that's staring us in the face; make it your job to put truth in 1st place.

OPEN UP to the goodness of GOD; put it solidly in your heart; use it in your life every day, knowing with GOD's goodness it will be impossible to stray.

OPEN UP to the wisdom of GOD; HIS wisdom is something we should never fear, in the end HE promises to wipe away every tear.

OPEN UP to the **LOVE OF GOD**; a love we should carry for everyone we come in contact with; is a commandment Jesus made perfectly clear, so keep your hearts happy refuse fear.

OPEN UP to the peace that HIS wisdom possesses; rest assured of passing all GOD'S test; know that you will be highly blessed.

OPEN UP to not sinning; each day is a new beginning; working hard for the team that will be winning.

OPEN UP to HIS **ALMIGHTY BLESSINGS,** they are plentiful for all to see! **PRAISE HIM! THANK HIM! FOR ALL HE DOES FOR YOU AND ME!!**

Amen

John 1: 1-5

MORE PRECIOUS
THAN GOLD

Throughout the ages, mankind has searched for riches, **mining for gold** only to be disappointed because it **did nothing for their soul**.

Man thinks if they are rich their worries will be gone; oh LORD that thought is truly wrong!

The scriptures say, **"What is a man that gains the whole world and loses his own soul"?** That man is loss spiritually and totally confused, giving your life to CHRIST will eliminate your soul being abused.

Closeness to GOD is something gold cannot buy; obtaining the wisdom HE left for us, we all must try.

Loving one another is more precious than gold; you cannot buy the love of family nor friends; they will love you from the beginning to the very end; they will be with you through thick and thin.

Integrity cannot be bought or sold; it is a part of one's mind and their soul; integrity is part of JESUS' make up, a gift to envelop for our spirits to develop.

We all possess riches my sisters and brothers; don't be confused by the type of riches that don't resemble gold; the greatest riches of all are buried deep in our souls.

Amen

Matthew 16:26

GREED

Greed is a word that is negative indeed; GOD has told us HE will provide for all our needs.

Greed is a self-inflicted action which will surely find one without GOD's grand protection.

Greed takes and takes, never giving to those in need; always wanting more, not having a clue of what's in store for a greedy mind and soul; lacking GOD's gracious and ultimate control.

Greed brings a false sense of security with riches on earth; there are truths that cannot be bought; no matter what we were taught.

Greed is a thought, an action that breeds selfishness; brewing a feeling of not caring of nothing, no one but you without compassion; the scriptures say that is not what GOD is about.

WITHOUT GREED there is an automatic trust that our creator will provide for us with a substance of helping others; while on this earth we must help others because **IN GOD WE TRUST**.

Nothing materialistic will assist us in our transition from life to death; which includes all materialistic things and all wealth.

With this poem I must say, **REPLACE GREED WITH GIVING TO THOSE IN NEED; THIS IS PLEASING TO GOD INDEED!!!**

Amen

1 Timothy 6:10
Matthew 25:42-46

BORROWED TIME

We are on borrowed time since our birth; GOD created all of us knowing how long we have on earth; HE has known before our birth.

There is a record of all we do; that goes for me and you; recorded in the Book of Life; judgment comes only from **GOD ALMIGHTY;**

Created from dust with GOD'S words; HIS words we must surely trust; the universe and all living things were created with the power of HIS words; they all are powerful and **WE ALL SHOULD OBSERVE**.

Use the borrowed time to give our Creator glory and praise; walk in HIS light and never be afraid.

Everything we own is on borrowed time; the control of our spiritual soul is all we have; do your best and know life is a spiritual test.

GOD knew when HE created us, our time was short; only HE knows the day, the hour and the minute life is over; stand up for the righteousness and become a lover of HIS word.

Use the borrowed time to give our **CREATOR GLORY AND PRAISE**; walk in the light with your heads held high; look forward to the day when none of us will cry!

Amen

Psalms 89:47

DISSAPPOINT THE DEVIL

Disappointing the devil is a sure way to make it to heaven; we all know the devil was kicked out of heaven never to return; what he wants for us is in hell to burn.

GOD has given us the power and strength to study HIS instructions; the evil one wants us to cause total destruction.

The Bible was left for all to read; understanding GOD's words and putting them into action means we all can succeed.

Praise GOD deep within and rebuke all sin; the devil gets mad; because of that we should be glad; the evil one is dangerous and truly sad.

We know JESUS CHRIST disappointed the evil one; showed us and told us it could be done; when we live our lives according to the scriptures we have won.

Study GOD's words, put them into action in all we do; rewards will be bountiful for all GOD'S servants; peace will overcome the turmoil of the world; IN THE END EVIL WILL NEVER WIN.

Amen.

Matthew 4:1
James 4:7

REST ASSURED

REST with the assurance of GOD's grace and love; His instructions are sent from the Heavens above.

REST assured when we sleep at night, when we awake there is a spiritual fight; fight to keep our spirits right by totally trusting in GOD morning noon and night.

REST assured the scriptures are true; protection from evil comes deep within; knowing our HEAVENLY FATHER in the end will surely win.

REST assured GOD is our KING; HE will provide us with all good things; **REST ASSURED JESUS IS OURS**; GOD Almighty gave HIM a great and awesome power.

REST assured as we walk in GOD's light; HE will uphold us and protect us in every fight;

REST assured we all can change; change can come in all types of range; never let up with GOD's spirit within; it's a way for evil to jump right in.

REST assured as life goes on speaking positive about our FATHER is a testament to our beliefs; GOD gives us solace and relief.

REST assured in all we do, our Heavenly Father is our protection; we don't have to worry about anything, **STAYING TRUE TO OUR UNDENIABLE KING.**

Amen

Hebrew 10:22-24

TIGHTEN UP!

Tighten up your heart, mind, and soul; put all your trust in GOD Almighty whom has undeniable control.

Tighten up on studying GOD'S words; they are strong and truthful; imbed them deeply in your soul; do what it says, with your actions be bold and you will find yourself surrounded by GOD's greatest control.

Tighten up on the way we treat family and friends; with the goodness of GOD we can't help but win; win their love and affection when we treat them with love; GOD's wisdom will never be a retraction.

Tighten up your thoughts each and every day; when negativism attacks remember to immediately pray.

Tighten up with helping those that are in need; do it from the heart, worry not; for we will never experience the lack of anything we need.

Tighten up your relationship with GOD Almighty; HE is the only ONE that can help us before we depart**; TOTALLY TRUSTING HIM IS EXTREMELY SMART.**

Amen

Psalm 143:8

LEAN ON GOD!

Whatever we go through we should always lean on GOD; HIS wisdom is grand, know it and believe it from deep in our heart; leaning on HIM is stress free, that's the way we should want it to be!

GOD makes no mistakes; HE is perfect in all HE does; **KNOW IT! BELIEVE IT! SIMPLY BECAUSE IT IS TRUE!**

Lean on our Heavenly FATHER for all our needs; HE has told us throughout the scriptures **HE IS THE ONE INDEED**!!

When trials and tribulations come upon us; be happy and know GOD will work it out in HIS way and in HIS time; just lean on HIM and everything will be just fine.

Lean on GOD in all that we do; HE is the only one that can take us through; take us through the rocky roads of life and lessen the blow of torment and strife;

BELIEVE IT BECAUSE IT'S TRUE, IT'S TRUE, IT'S TRUE!!!

Amen

Psalm 37:39-40

FAITH SAYS

Faith says: Trust your LORD GOD all your days in the land of the living.

Faith says: Substance of things hoped for, the evidence of things not seen.

Faith says: The world was framed by the word of GOD, so things which are seen were not made of things which appear.

Faith says: Without it, it is impossible to please GOD; for him that cometh to GOD must believe HE is.

Faith says: Those that believe and trust GOD Almighty will be rewarded to those who diligently seek HIM.

Faith says: Check out Noah, a man who moved with fear; obeying GOD's every word, built an ark designed by GOD and became heir to righteousness.

Faith says: Seek ye first the kingdom of GOD and HIS righteousness, and all our needs will be met.

Faith says: Whatsoever things you shall desire when you pray, believe them and you shall have them.

So, my sisters and brother continuously seek the righteousness of GOD's word; believe and trust totally in HIM and only HIM.

Amen!

Luke 17:6

LAST DAYS

Living in the last days, the signs are here for all to see; it's evidenced in the four corners of the earth; awful things are happening, parents are killing their children before birth.

Tornadoes, earthquakes, mudslides, sinkholes, floods, tsunamis, with volcanoes exploding all over the universe; a sign from GOD wanting our attention; **GIVE HIM PRAISE.** GOD ALMIGHTY is the ultimate inventor and need not our permission for HIS ultimate transition.

Murderous rampages are on the rise; people killing people come as no surprise; we see incarnated evil in folks, only to get worse as time continues on; there is a **RIGHTEOUS SAVIOR THAT WANTS OUR SOULS**; let HIM have it and takeover with righteous control.

The scriptures have foretold these days over and over again; reading the bible only demonstrates how much GOD loves us; preparing us for these awful times; we have a source of protection; march in the heavenly direction is a blessed spiritual correction.

Wrapping our souls in the amour of faith; giving JESUS HIS praise will keep us strong during these last days we all will face!

Amen

Matthew 24:7
Luke 21:11

NO PEACE FOR THE WICKED

There cannot be peace for the wicket in GOD's land; HE has made that perfectly clear, all of us better understand.

The wicked ones are doing everything against GOD's will; doing all sort of things for a cheap thrill; walking GOD's earth seeking to maim, steal and kill.

Their souls are in turmoil; their minds are confused; they are the ones that constantly abuse.

GOD has told us throughout the scriptures, **THE WICKED WILL PERISH;** also the LORD knows the way of the righteous; they shall inherit the earth – what a contrast; brothers and sisters the difference between the wicked and the righteous cannot be masked.

The wicked rebels against GOD's instructions; seek for themselves and mankind's total destruction; those that fear the LORD shall have favor and security in the land of the living, said GOD; **SEEK HIM AND NEVER DEPART!!!**

Amen

Proverbs 11:5

THE INNER SPIRIT

The inner man is the true spirit; what's on the inside must come out that is without a doubt; goodness and evil will expose itself from the inside out; the character of that man is what it's all about.

Peace within can be felt in our daily lives and all we want to represent; no need to worry with peace within; a good clean spirit is what GOD commends.

Trusting in GOD is an inner spiritual thing; it shows itself without having to tell others you walk with righteousness in your being; believing and trusting in GOD is a mighty attribute; when doing so we give GOD the highest salute.

The inner spirit is either good or bad; when it's good GOD smiles and keeps us close and protected in HIS hands.

The outer man can fool others; the inner man is the one GOD knows; GOD cannot be fooled with the outer man's soul.

Strength, peace and grace are attributes from the spirit of CHRIST; solid traits; nourish them and keep them close as we walk the narrow path to see our HEAVENLY FATHER once we leave this earthly land.

Amen

2 Corinthians 4:16
Psalm 51:10-12

GOD HAS THE MASTER PLAN

We can plan our life all we want; what GOD has planned will ultimately be in our best interest; representing GOD while we live on this earth in GOD's land; be grateful and thankful for whatever HE has planned.

Don't get discouraged when things don't go our way; GOD's plan is the better plan for all of us on earth as we live on GOD's land.

Following CHRISTS' walk on this earth is for a reason; things will change just like the seasons; know that we all have a special talent; finding it and using it brings the soul total satisfaction.

GOD will lead us only if we listen, to heights unknown; as we travel through this world ultimately we will see what GOD has in store for you and me.

We must do the very best in everything we do; that's how our spirit will lead us to the mountain HE has planned before we were born; it is certainly a way to be mindful of HIS wonderful throne.

Obeying GOD's Will is a satisfaction to HIM; HE knows what the master plan is.

When putting all our trust and faith in GOD, the path will lead us to a place where we belong; that path will be tough, it will make us strong; **WHEN DOING GOD'S WILL WE CANNOT GO WRONG!!!**

Amen.

2 Peter 3:9

WISDOM

GOD ALMIGHTY has the wisdom for young and old; all races in different places; **THE KNOWLEDGE OF WHAT IS TRUE;** GOD has given it to me and you!

Man can gain wisdom by reading the bible; following GOD's direct instructions; they are written to lessen our troubles in all situations; wisdom can be learned for all denominations.

Wisdom comes from listening to the wise people of our day; they have already experienced life and death; know the difference between truth and lies; will tell us all how to survive.

With wisdom there are a lot of things we don't have to experience; wise ones will tell us the outcome in the beginning; listening is a way of winning.

GOD ALMIGHTY is all wise and the scriptures are full of wisdom; and stories of the unwise; only the truth prevails with absolutely no lies!

We should pray for wisdom constantly; with it we will save ourselves from foolish obstacles that don't need to be; with GOD's wisdom it will allow us all to see!

Amen

Proverbs 4:7
Proverbs 16:16

NO LIMITS

With GOD ALMIGHTY there are no limits of what HE can do for me and you; those who know HIM and believe in HIM know it is true.

HE can move mountains and HE can part the sea; simply because GOD is limitless when it comes to you and me.

Keep your faith strong in the mighty works of GOD; HE has shown there are no limits when we keep HIM strong in our hearts.

CREATOR of the universe and the solar system too; GOD'S miracles are still in effect; believe it because it is a **TRUE FACT!**

There are no limits on the ***RIGHTEOUS ALMIGHTY GOD;*** we must praise HIM and keep HIS spirit deep in our hearts.

It is so clear that GOD is always near; never having to fear or wanting for our needs to be met; HE will take good care of us and that too is a **TRUE FACT!**

Never think GOD cannot perform miracles today; as HE cradle us in HIS loving arms never, ever wanting us to stray.

Amen

Ephesians 3:20

GPS (GLOBAL POSITIONING SYSTEM)

We all think the GPS will get us to a location, don't be fooled regarding this systems destination; the following is the true GPS, now listen to this:

GOD'S PERFECT SOLUTIONS
GOD'S PRESENT SECURITY
GODS' PRONOUNCED SPIRIT
GOD'S PLEASING SPONTANEITY
GOD'S PLENTIFUL SURROUNDINGS
GOD'S PRETTY SPECIAL
GOD'S PROFOUND SUPREMANCY
GOD'S PERSONAL SOLVER
GOD'S PLAIN SCRIPTURES
GOD'S PRICELESS SANCTUARY

So when we depend on man's GPS to deliver us to our next destination; remember the spiritual GPS; it will lead us to a righteous revelation.

Amen

James 1:17

SURVEILLANCE

Cameras are everywhere we go, at the stop signals, on the streets, in every store; in folks homes surveillance are being put up to watch out for thieves and peoples stuff.

Phones are being tapped, Uncle Sam know where you go with or without a map; surveillance is everywhere we go; think about it long enough you will feel trapped.

GOD ALMIGHTY is the greatest surveillance of all; we cannot escape GOD'S presence; HE knows what we are thinking, knows what is in our hearts; HE cannot be tricked, understand that from the start.

Fooling people on earth about who you really are have no credence; man's judgment has no say whether we go to Heaven or hell; GOD's surveillance is the one that matters; after this life it will surely tell.

Watch what you do, think and feel; the surveillance of GOD is ALMIGHTY and real; HIS surveillance will never go on the blink. AGAIN, BE VERY CAREFUL OF WHAT YOU DO AND WHAT YOU THINK!!!

Amen.

Jeremiah 16:17
Song of Solomon 5:12
Exodus 5:12

SELF RESTRICTIONS

RESTRICT ourselves from negative thoughts; it does no good and will cause us to be misunderstood.

RESTRICT ourselves from people who despise the truth; those people will walk and talk with evil deep within; carrying around the chain of sin.

RESTRICT ourselves from wronging others; when we do it makes us jealous of our sisters and brothers.

RESTRICT ourselves from holding grudges; it kills our spirits as we try to be the judge of others; it's not our job to hold a grudge or to judge.

RESTRICT ourselves from being selfish and greedy; we should all help those who are obviously needy.

RESTRICT ourselves from evil thoughts; it will only bring about evil deeds; none of which we need.

BE UNRESTRICTED IN DOING WHAT IS RIGHT ACCORDING TO SCRIPTURE; IT WILL ENHANCE OUR SPIRITS AND MAKE OUR FUTURES BRIGHT.

Amen

Colossians 3:25
Acts 7:26-27

SEED PLANTING

When planting a garden we decide what type of seeds will be planted; we work the earth getting rid of weeds; fertilizing the land before we plant the seeds; we watch it grow and when it's ripe, we retrieve it with pure delight.

So with this poem I must say:

PLANT SEEDS OF INTEGRITY
PLANT SEEDS OF TRUTH
PLANT SEEDS OF FAITH
PLANT SEEDS OF HAPPINESS
PLANT SEEDS OF HUMILITY
PLANT SEEDS OF EMPATHY
PLANT SEEDS OF FORGIVENESS
PLANT SEEDS OF CHARITY
PLANT SEEDS OF LOVE
PLANT SEEDS OF TOLERANCE
PLANT SEEDS OF PEACE ...

What we sow, nourish and plant is what we will surely reap and get back; send out good so good comes back; and my sisters and brothers you will live extremely happy and that's a fact.

AMEN

Isaiah 59:21
Isaiah 60:21
2 Corinthians 9:10

PEACE

When we trust totally in our ALMIGHTY GOD, peace will embrace mind, body and soul; it cannot be bought, borrowed or stolen; that type of peace is from GOD and it is golden.

All types of obstacles will come our way; but when at peace with the LORD, HE will protect us and show us the way.

Peace knows GOD is our protector; staying true to HIS words lead us to a righteous connector; connecting with the good, spreading GOD's words **BRING ABOUT A PEACE THAT CANNOT BE DISTURBED**.

Crazy is the world all in itself, getting further away from GOD's instructions; with the knowledge and wisdom from GOD ALMIGHTY it will lessen what the evil one seeks, which is total destruction.

Being at peace in everything we do only proves who we bow down to; the Prince of Peace is a mighty good spirit; it's one we want every second of each day; It's what we should ask of the LORD as we continuously pray!

Amen

2 Corinthians 13:11
James 3:18

A MUSTARD SEED

A tiny seed the scriptures say is all we need to have **_faith_** in GOD and HIS SON JESUS; then why is it we get stressed and downright depressed?

Believe and know GOD'S words are true; they bring about a peace and happiness in all we do.

GOD has told us with **_faith_** we can move mountains and drink of wealth from HIS fountains.

With **_faith_** there is nothing GOD cannot do; HE has shown us over and over again; acknowledge it, testify to family and friends; keep believing; it will surely happen again.

If it's only a tiny seed of **_faith_** HE asks from us; adopt an avocado seed of **_faith_** and trust; it's the greatest way to deal with life, it alleviates a lot of stress and strife.

Just know this, GOD is real and HIS words are true; believe it, know it; feel it in your heart, mind and soul; a small mustard seed of **_faith_** will give GOD the highest of praise; for every good thing that happens to you, you will be absolutely amazed!!!

Amen

Matthew 17:20

ELDERLY FLIGHT

If GOD sees fit we will age; with time our bodies and minds will age as well; certain parts will cease to work while other parts of the body and mind will be just fine.

Elders think about it all the time; will our children be there for us during these difficult times? Loving us unconditional as age takes its toll? Will they be there with love in their soul?

Will they remember when we were young how we struggled to keep them strong and secure as time moved on? Will they have the same love for us as age progresses and time continues on as we wait for GOD to take us to HIS throne?

Will our children be there for us during our last stages on this earth? To love us and help us as we did from their birth? Will they help us from their hearts, be there for us before our bodies depart?

WELL IF THEY DON'T, IT'S OKAY! Pleasing GOD is most important in every way is what we will say as ageing take us through another day; knowing GOD's love will keep us and protect us in every way!

Amen

Ephesians 6:1-4
Exodus 20:12

GOD'S CHARACTER

OUR FATHER'S character is unquestionably superior to mankind; HIS character is one we should seek for ourselves and pray that we find.

OUR FATHER'S character is filled with truth; we should shout about it through the roof; HIS character is awesome; with the scriptures we have undeniable proof.

OUR FATHER'S character is filled with pure love; HE seeks for us to do what is right, so we can make it to Heaven above.

OUR FATHER'S character is strong and just; HE allows us free will to see whom we will trust.

OUR FATHER'S character is gentle and filled with grace; with faith HE will protect us as we run life's race.

OUR FATHER'S character is the greatest of all; that's why JESUS came to show us we may stumble, but we will not fall.

OUR FATHER'S character has anger and wrath; it's a side we should never want to experience; HE is capable of showing HIS displeasure and those things are complicated to measure.

STUDY GOD'S CHARACTER; incorporate it into your spirit; allow truth, peace, love, charity, and forgiveness to enter your spiritual space; as we run for our lives in this spiritual race.

Amen.

2 Timothy 3:16-17

PERSONAL RELATIONSHIPS

Most of us seek personal relationships with a woman or a man; say we want a companion to grow old with and walk the beaches on beautiful white sand.

We look, we seek to find that special one; looking for that soul mate is something most of us can relate as we go out on a date.

The first personal relationship we all should chase is the one with GOD ALMIGHTY; knowing HE is a good great spirit without a human face.

That relationship is a spiritual one that cultivates our souls and our minds; to get closer to GOD we should praise HIM all the time.

HE tells us clear as can be, "**Seek Ye First THE KINGDOM OF GOD**", when we do, it will make all other relationships stronger and simpler from the start.

A personal relationship with our **FATHER ABOVE** will enhance our prayers and protect us during difficult times; it's pleasing to GOD as HIS children of faith; trusting and believing in HIS words in every way; **SO I SAY, STAYED PRAYED UP EACH SECOND OF EVERYDAY!!!**

Amen

Matthew 6:33

MODEL

MODEL YOURSELVES WITH GOD'S WORDS; show it off with grandeur and grace; live life showing off GOD's goodness in all we will face.

MODEL ON THE RUNWAY OF LIFE; knowing there are things we all will sacrifice; when modeling for GOD we should never have to think twice.

MODEL WITH STRENGTH AND PRAISE; others will see GOD in your beautiful eyes in or out of your gaze.

MODEL HIS WORDS THROUGH YOUR ACTIONS; ignore negative distractions; when we model with GOD in our minds, life will remain clear most of the time.

MODEL WITH TRUTH AND INTEGRITY IN YOUR WALK; for when we do GOD is happy for HIS creation is pleasing HIM too!

MODEL WITH HAPPINESS AND GRATEFULNESS IN YOUR STRUT; for it is contagious to those that don't believe nor trust.

MODEL WITH HEADS HELD HIGH; model with your backs straight looking up towards the sky; because modeling for our SAVIOR will bring good rewards for all to see; those rewards comes directly from GOD.

Amen

Jeremiah 32:19

INJUSTICE

It's becoming quite evident in these last days, injustice is all over the world it's really clear; a lot of people are living in fear.

People are being murdered because of their beliefs; around the world there appears to be no relief.

Groups of people are walking the universe seeking to kill; it looks like they may get away with murderous deeds; those groups of people GOD's words they do not heed!

Doing these ungodly and evil things; brings about strife to others of all things; unfortunately for them the judgment will come from GOD above; it be will swift and quick; believe me sisters and brothers it will be harsh and direct; the scriptures tell us that is a fact.

GOD ALMIGHTY is the judge of all; it is guaranteed the evil on this earth will surely fall.

Know this and believe; it is true; justice from GOD is the greatest justice of all; those that do not obey will surely fall!

Amen

Job 16:17

GOING, GOING, GONE!!!

When judgment comes from our HEAVENLY FATHER, it will be quick and precise without a doubt; the work is done right here on earth; it started from our birth.

HE has given instructions for us to follow; going to heaven to be with our FATHER; we should strive every second of each day; always obeying HIS commandments without delay.

Going through life is guaranteed trials and tribulations; dealing with life in positive and grateful ways will help us through those tiring days.

Going through sickness and illness, knowing GOD can heal and bring about a wellness in our minds, bodies and soul; we should rejoice and call out HIS name mightily and bold.

Going after the goodness of GOD will delight HIM before we depart; studying HIS words, putting them into action gives us the roadmap to HIS KINGDOM; watch out for the evil ones trap!

Time is going and moves quickly right along; before we know it the time is gone!

SO, AS WE ARE MOVING AND GOING ON; DO GOOD AND WHAT IS RIGHT BEFORE THE TIME IS GOING, GOING, GONE!!!

Amen

1 Peter 4:17